CAN HE PRAY FOR ME

PRAY FOR ME

(Instead of Preying on Me)

I0519353

BRANDI PAYNE

www.TrueVinePublishing.org

Can He Pray for Me
Brandi Payne

Published by
True Vine Publishing Co
810 Dominican Dr. Ste 103
Nashville, TN 37228
www.TrueVinePublishing.org

ISBN: 978-1-962783-16-3 Paperback
ISBN: 978-1-962783-17-0 eBook

Printed in the United States—First Printing

ACKNOWLEDGMENTS

To all my God-sent angels who left this earth way too soon on my spiritual journey and who encouraged and uplifted me, each one has a special place in my heart.

To my great-grandmother, Marie Dowlen, my great aunt Carline Payne, my uncle Robert L. Moseley, my special godmother, Angela Turner, and my two special friends, Maria Reasha Taylor and Talisha Smith.

Special bonus thank you to a very powerful woman I met on social media in mid-July 2022. She had a profound message, and her timing was impeccable. She was just what I prayed for; she had knowledge, wisdom, and spiritual insight. She transformed my mind, body, and soul and advised me to never settle for less. I took her 7-hour course. She proved to me that men are incapable of love, and that I should not look for love outside of myself. She saved my physical, mental, and spiritual life. She is called the Queen Maker, saving women's lives all over the world.

Princella Clark YouTube channel: the high-powered podcast, author of the 5 Components of Love

The game 41 Shades of Men

TABLE OF CONTENTS

TURNING YOUR PAIN INTO POWER
AFFIRMATIONS FOR THE SOUL

"My steps are ordered through my pain. (Think about what life is teaching in this critical moment).

My pain has challenged me to be set free and whole. (I encourage myself).

My pain brought me the gift of forgiving myself.

I have power and victory over pain.

Allow pain to bring you to peace, not pieces. (Only you have the power to totally heal yourself).

WISDOM IS THE MASTER KEY TO OPEN FUTURE DOORS

1. Power - Walking in Kingdom Feminine Authority
2. Prayer - Pray with Attention About Everything Before Making Decisions
3. Pronouncement - Proclaim and Declare God's Divine Feminine Word Over Your Life
4. Position - Make the Right Connections in the Right Season
5. Purpose - Find Out the Difference Between Purpose and Passion. Purpose is Fulfilling; Passion is Temporary to Draw a Certain Crowd. There are Too Many People in the World That Are Out of Kingdom Order and Assignment.
6. Process - Trust Your Godly Intuition; Allow Discernment to be Your Spiritual Guide
7. Patience - Wait for What is Good to be Manifested. If Anything Appears, Make Sure You Check What Spirit is Behind the Scenes. It's Easy to be Fooled by Godly Intentions.
8. Pattern - Change Your Lifestyle if it is Not Aligned with Your True Purpose
9. Perspective - It's All About Your View and Outlook on Life. How Do You See Things Versus Reality
10. Preparation - Training Grounds to Study Yourself. Make Sure You Have No Cracks in Your Foundation for the Enemy to Creep In
11. Peace - In Knowing You Have Made the Right Decision. No Doubt Or Worry Of Past Familiar Spirits Coming Back
12. Proverbs 31: Know Your Worth. For Your Price is Far Above Rubies. It Attracts Demons.

QUEEN SUPREME CODE
BY BRANDI PAYNE

- Queens are natural-born leaders.
- Queens always hold their heads up high.
- Queens make righteous, conscientious decisions.
- Queens have wisdom, special gifts, and powers.
- Queens know their worth at all times.
- Queens are spiritually connected to God.
- Queens do not settle for less.
- Queens have the power to command a room.
- Queens love themselves.
- Queens are responsible and take accountability.
- Queens get respect everywhere they go.
- Queens are healed and whole from negative energy.
- Queens don't have competition.
- Queens don't carry a jealous spirit. Every woman is celebrated no matter what level she is on.
- Queens are life givers and life savers.
- Queens are at peace.
- Queens are successful in everything they touch.
- Queens know when to walk away from anyone who does not serve a righteous purpose & have sexual freedom
- Queens are wealthy in every aspect of life (spiritually, mentally, physically, and financially).
- Queens play chess, not checkers.

INTRODUCTION

This book explores victims and villains, predators, and prey, demonstrating how someone you admire can manipulate your good values. Consider this: How can a person you've chosen to prioritize end up deceiving you? The answer is simple. This dark and deceptive spirit will engage with you where you are, diverting and duping you.

Many girls fall into the trap of seduction, believing it will lead to a happy relationship, but it often results in trouble. Some guys present themselves as virtuous, attracting good girls. They exploit emotions and loyalty, even employing religion to deceive. They may attend church, pray with you, and appear genuinely nice—all to prevent you from discerning their true motives.

Many men are naturally predatory, but they excel at concealing it, asserting they are pursuing you. They set girls up for significant disappointment in relationships. They cheat because, as their needs change, they seek someone else to fulfill those needs, whether it's for sex, money, or a place to stay. Regardless of how well you treat them, you become the prey.

I'm here to unveil the not-so-great truth about guys and their behavior. As a spiritual writer, I aim to assist girls in being confident, free, and aware of guys who aim to confuse, hurt, impoverish, and make them feel worthless and weak. Girls may not realize it, but they were born complete and free. It's only when the world interferes with their minds, bodies, and souls that they become slaves to the system and feel defeated.

Ever wonder why girls worldwide deal with similar guys, regardless of their race, who cheat, control, and harm them? It's quite perplexing. There's something dark and unsettling about predatory men, and more girls are discovering that they were never genuinely loved; they were merely being used. They throw around the word 'love' combined with religion to get what they want in bed.

Many girls have lost themselves in serious relationships with bad guys. It's time for girls to take control and lead. I wrote this book because, even when the truth is apparent, girls still believe they can pray and transform a bad guy while desiring marriage or a relationship, despite the unfavorable odds.

This book is rated S (Spiritual)
: survival of spiritual warfare
: survival of spiritual suicide

As a revelation spiritual author, I can guide you, if you permit, on a journey towards freedom and redemption. This message is for queens, urging them to unveil the factors hindering their spiritual growth. Women have been conditioned under a patriarchal matrix to submit to male dominance, becoming sacrificial lambs for male survival, even in toxic situations. This conditioning places women beneath a false system, hindering their spiritual progress. The earth has suffered various hardships, such as famine, wars, earthquakes, tsunamis, and the rapid spread of diseases. The imbalance has affected family, children, animal life, and death, leading the planet away from homeostasis. Demonic spirits have exploited natural resources, reshaping the world.

Due to this gender war, men and women are not seen as equal partners in the game of life. Men traditionally have had spiritual and economic advantages over women. Religion has reinforced male leadership, and an entirely male government has mandated marriage for women to receive benefits. This book draws inspiration from the 1974 Equal Credit Act and the year women gained financial freedom and independence. Spiritually, it highlights how evil men placed women at a disadvantage, suppressing their true divine nature and purpose in choosing a partner. Women endured abuse, rape, and being treated as property. The question arises: Was this righteous, or do men feel a moral obligation to control and punish women for extended periods in relationships?

Women were silenced, conditioned to love everything and everyone else but themselves. This explains why women often feel empty, seeking validation externally. Only when a woman loves herself can she become whole and make better decisions.

The question posed is whether, knowing the truth about male nature, a woman would still desire marriage, given the significant chance it might not last beyond a season.

DISCLAIMER FOR THE PUSH BACK WOMAN

As an author and spiritual advisor, my goal, purpose, and ultimate gift is to rescue women from toxic relationships and to guide them toward freedom, wholeness, and life beyond pain, trauma, and heartache. My message emanates from a place of love and healing. While I teach about evil spirits and spiritual warfare, it is crucial for women to understand the harsh truth about male nature and biology. This knowledge is essential for women to navigate the complexities of relationships and avoid mistreatment.

This book serves as a warning for some women, offering valuable insights into potential dangers. Others may interpret it negatively, especially if they have positive male figures in their lives, such as pastors, fathers, sons, brothers, nephews, and cousins. It is important to acknowledge and address red flags, even among the men deemed 'good.' A glance at the news reveals crimes against women committed by individuals with destructive behaviors, highlighting the urgency of this message.

The ongoing gender war poses significant risks to women, young girls, and children. Approximately 80% of males exhibit toxic traits and may not be suitable for marriage or relationships. This demonic behavior permeates various aspects of society, including government, law enforcement, religion, social media, music, and culture. While there are approximately 20% decent men, it is crucial to approach this cautiously, considering diverse sexual orientations. Women have prayed for centuries for a good man, yet many remain single, prompting reflection on the scarcity of men saving themselves for marriage.

This message is not meant to encourage settling; rather, it serves as a cautionary reminder for women facing challenges in finding suitable partners.

To women who might find my bold warning offensive, let me clarify the types of males I am advising against. It is important to remember that wolves often come disguised as sheep, so pay attention to the spirit. Have you encountered or been in a relationship with males exhibiting traits such as lying, abuse, or manipulation? The reality is that all males may possess these traits to varying degrees. Whether murderers, criminals, narcissists, religious demons, rapists, sex traffickers, drug dealers, drug users, alcoholics, or individuals with other negative characteristics, it is crucial to be vigilant and discerning in relationships.

CLIFFHANGER

The question arises: can he pray for me instead of preying on me? Are males good partners? Consider your past, present, and future experiences.

Will you believe the 80% or higher, the majority of males who may fall below average? Or will you hold onto false hope, praying to find the 1% rare breed, the unicorns of men? By the 80%, I mean that a significant number of men lack emotional intelligence. They may not have invested in personal development to foster a healthy, successful relationship with a woman. In the world, women often run households while men enjoy male privilege as the perceived heads or leaders in a patriarchal system. Women have evolved beyond the role of a housewife and deserve equal partnerships. To protect male ego and avoid violent dominance, women have lowered themselves, often staying in the background due to fear.

The question persists: where are the 1%—whole, healthy, decent, righteous men who bring more than just financial stability? If this relationship dynamic weren't an issue, the world wouldn't be in such disarray, and women wouldn't wait for years to meet a good man. The harsh reality is that the majority of women may not find a good man or husband. If desperately desired, one could settle, but there are plenty of wicked ones to choose from. Males harboring wicked spirits rule the world, submitting to phallic worship, displaying a pimp spirit, acting as entitled narcissists, and being high-value tricksters with money and power to control women. This results in women being contaminated with spirit poisons, giving birth to a generation of rebellious, out-of-control human beings.

Ask yourself: how is this a successful relationship for a woman dealing with multiple spirits that come to conquer and destroy her? After reading this book, each woman will draw her own conclusions. Some may be triggered, agreeing with the truth but clinging to the hope that males will change. Others will view it positively, taking it as a warning that could potentially save their lives. As a woman, you have the power. Ask yourself: do I want a ring just for show, risking misery in marriage, or do I want my rights and total freedom over my life? The choice is yours.

CHAPTER 1:
KNOWING YOUR WORTH

Proverbs 26:11: As a dog that returns to its vomit, so is a fool who repeats his foolishness)

Doing the same thing over and over and expecting different results equals insanity.

So many women tend to allow family, friends, social media, and demonic men to define their value and self-worth. In doing so, they may inadvertently disrespect themselves and allow others, especially men, to take advantage of them. Both men and women who prioritize instant gratification often find their own value depreciating. Toxic men, in particular, can treat women poorly, turning their bodies into receptacles for negative energy that may break them down into submission. If true submission were natural, it wouldn't require force or control.

The core message is that women lose power and strength when connecting with the wrong individuals. The challenge lies in the difficulty women face in choosing better partners, as all males may have hidden motives until they achieve their desires. They often present a facade, putting forth their best behavior initially. It's important not to misconstrue the statement that "all men" possess these traits. Rather, when examining global data, experiences, statistics, history, and patterns, many women have faced similar challenges.

The stark reality, often overlooked, is that over 90% of men are in prison. While it's crucial not to generalize, the majority may exhibit similar characteristics, making the rare minority harder to find. A man who engages in promiscuity solely for attention can be particularly dangerous, lacking morals, standards, and values. Denying such temptations requires confidence and strength.

The advice for women is to redirect their focus onto themselves. Instead of allowing external influences to shape their worth, women should prioritize self-improvement and personal development. This self-focused approach empowers women to make better choices and build a strong foundation for their lives.

They should focus on their education, having their own home, and their own money. Never put all your hope and trust in a man. He will fail you every time. Remember: nothing lasts forever. Your freedom is based on how you move and make decisions.

He could drain and leave you with nothing. Many women have had to learn this lesson the hard way. At the end of the day, ownership is the key. Nobody can take anything from you if your name is the only name on the policy. Think smart.

Men use women to help them come up with good credit all the time. If a man doesn't have anything going on for him, he is very dangerous. He is looking for a victim to prey on. Don't allow a man to pump you full of babies because the majority do not stay and help you raise them. The ones who have a lot of children are reckless with their bodies.

Men have marked their territory like dogs. It's all a game to slow a woman down. Biologically, women are ahead of men. Women are more mature, mentally, physically, emotionally, sexually, and financially. Think about it: if the man was the head, why does he need so much help? Do your research and homework on male nature, and brain studies show they lack a lot of chromosomes. Scientific studies show that males should not be leaders because they are so reckless and deficient, and they only use one side of their brains.

And they are not good relationship partners because they are so needy and codependent on women and male approval and validation. I am not making this up to bash men. This is all factual information that can be proven publicly. One of men's biggest fears is being alone. Hence, they often push relationships on women, urging them to lower their standards just to have a companion. However, the man is unlikely to provide what the woman has been praying for. Males often sell women dreams, lies, and fairy tales to fulfill their own needs. Women inherently possess value and have always been the focus of attention due to beauty standards. This is why men employ power, money, and flashy cars just to be noticed by women.

Many women may not be aware that men harbor jealousy and internal animosity, engaging in a perpetual, secret competition with women since the beginning of time. Consider this: why is it that whenever a man assumes power or leadership, he may risk everything to embezzle money, engage in sex, or commit sexual assault? This pattern extends to individuals holding high titles in religion and government, but even the average everyday man may exhibit similar tendencies.

Male's true nature has always been exposed for centuries, but women have always had a forgiving blind eye and refuse to give up on finding love and relationships that have brought her pain and trauma. Women don't have the same code of ethics that men have because women have been taught to stay and pray when all signs say leave. Some men will try to kill their partner if she leaves or breaks up with him because males are emotionally unstable. Women cry and yell.

Men rape and kill. That's a huge difference in genders, and in some cases, if children are involved, he makes his children's mother suffer a life of living hell or he just may have a bad influence and turn the children against their mother. The list goes on. You see the horror stories play out every day. Wicked males prey on women and innocent children. Males love young virgin girls who are gullible and naive. They know if they can control her body, they can control her mind. I have heard men say, "Do what I say, not what I do." Women are put on a high pedestal in life and society from birth because the woman is the superior gender–biology and science prove this 100%.

Women have been under oppression and a false system that has kept them out of the knowledge of their true nature and purpose for centuries. Women are the true natural-born leaders, which explains why men blame women for everything. When women know their worth, they will not put up with being mistreated, abused, and used just to say, "I have a man or look at my ring." Women have paid a harsh price because of their desire for love and companionship outside of themselves.

1 Corinthians 15:33 "Do not be deceived bad company ruins good morals"

But who is the bad company that women are keeping, wanting to marry, have children with, and entertain, causing pain, trauma, mental, emotional, and health issues?

Ask yourself this question: do you really want love or a form of love and would you still consider taking that risk if you knew the enemy is providing it?

CHAPTER 2:
LIVING IN TRUTH (LIT)

When a woman discovers who she truly is, there will be plenty of resources and benefits as she looks at the world. Even though men have powerful positions that were basically given to them like kings, presidents, pastors, and CEOs, everyone knows that the church would not exist if it were not for the women of the church spending their money, time, and effort to support men and the community.

This explains why there is always one male pastor assigned to 200 women and 3 men that attend church. That should say in your spirit that there is a huge problem in males, and most do not want to be decent human beings with morals, values, or standards. They just want to live a wild, reckless life, sleep with as many women as they can, and have lots of children with no accountability, and then on their deathbed ask for forgiveness.

Men don't go to church unless it benefits them. Women have been lied to and tricked in relationships because women are the only ones praying and long-suffering to get into one, but you would have to dig deeper on religion and male pathology to really get what I am saying. A lot of religious women and just women in general would rather be comforted with lies than to peel back the layers to discover the ugly truth about the opposite sex.

They just want to have a husband and a wife title for the world to see. Women are the true leaders behind the scenes in everything, especially at church and corporations. Men just show up or be present and take credit for doing nothing. Males know their true core nature. That's why they don't trust other males. They use women as tools to become successful.

Women are the most educated and responsible, and since they joined the workforce, women have proven to be better workers than men. A queen has to have a renewed restored mindset and vision to be set free from bondage. Women think they need men to validate them because they want to feel special and important, but God designed every woman different, unique, and alike because she carries a womb. It's time for women to learn the importance of womanhood.

Women were born with a healthy mind, body, heart, soul, and spirit, but when a demonic predator comes into her life, she loses her God-given power, and she will deny the truth—aka the red flags—just to be in a relationship, even if it's not going anywhere. Women are only in bondage because they deny the truth of who males really are.

They pretend and hide behind the good guy image until their real mask is revealed. All you have to do is look at all the statistics on divorce and see how ugly and crazy things can get. Some women have lost their lives being married to a demon. I have asked over a hundred women, "Would you get married again?" They all said no. Do not be deceived by godly intentions. Keep your heart guarded on who or what comes into your life. No more wasting time to become a slave woman. Have power and wisdom to stop this vicious cycle that you were never meant to be in. Take accountability for past mistakes, move on, don't look back, and be set free forever. Take your power back.

CHAPTER 3:
CALLING THE SHOTS
(IN YOUR SINGLENESS)

It's time for the real women of purpose to stand up and take your mind, heart, bodies, and souls back. You even have the power to take your sex back. Women have been programmed and brainwashed to give all their gifts away to men for free. Religion is the only institute that paints males to be good people and worthy of love and companionship, but real life shows a grim picture of heartache and setbacks that all fall back on the woman.

Someone doing good deeds in public and showing acts of kindness does not mean that they are marriage or relationship material. I really want you to step back and really think about what I am saying. It's time for women to quit giving away their life energy to demons. Be a queen boss, listen to key things that will trigger or throw off your discernment, speak up when it's time to move on, and never let anyone get in the way of your purpose.

Predators show up to hinder or slow you down. Learn to prepare, plan, possess and take charge and ownership of the life God has for you. Your path course can change quickly by yoking up with the wrong partner. Never settle for less or wait on anything or anybody to get themselves together. Women have worked hard to change their past mistakes but get robbed of that by giving predators a chance.

Ask yourself this question: why is it every time a woman gets out of a relationship with a man, she has to completely start over? The woman is trapped because she stays hoping the outcome will be different. The majority of males are liabilities, not assets. There is no real kingdom, growth, or showing of any fruits of the spirit. Some couples just look good on paper but are unequally yoked in the spirit, talents, or degrees and education.

Sometimes this is a smoke screen to look like you are a good person with morals, values, and standards. Males use sex as a weapon to sedate women, to keep them confused on where the relationship really stands because the majority of the time, it's only the woman that really wants the relationship to work out. He could be careless. Don't be fooled by charm.

Take the c away and you have the word harm. I didn't write this book to go hard on men. I wrote it to go hard on women, to tell and show them they're in a losing battle. There is a major crisis going on. Why do women have to help build up a man?

Most of them move into women's homes and take over, and the women are afraid to put them out. Some are reckless and get the woman and her children put out. Some of them quit their jobs because they want a woman to take care of them. We all know no one is perfect, but when you break down male pathology and their raw nature, you will see it's very dark, animalistic, and sinister.

Men do not see women as human. They only see things from a sexual point of view, and everything is transactional for them, where women are used as tools or objects to impress other men. There is total freedom in being single. It holds a power like no other. A woman can focus on herself without judgment or pressure. Being alone in power and being lonely, looking for someone to fill a void, are two different things. Do not allow anyone to live rent-free off your hard work and achievements who never benefited you.

CHAPTER 4:
NO WEAPON FORMED AGAINST YOU SHALL PROSPER

The desire of a woman's heart is to avoid being lied to, cheated on, or attacked. Many women may not fully realize the protection inherent in their singleness. This prompts spiritual reflection: could being with the wrong man serve as a weapon against a woman's mind, body, and soul? It's a thought-provoking consideration about the potential spiritual impact of choosing the right partner and recognizing the inherent safeguards in maintaining one's singleness.

Diabolical predator males seek out loyal women to attack in the spirit, drawing them into their world. It revolves around the predator's desires and intentions. They carry the weight of unresolved issues from broken relationships, continuously trying to manipulate the narrative in their favor.

These predators aim to gain control and waste a woman's time, employing various forms of abuse—verbal, mental, violence, and sexual abuse. No weapon formed exposes the evil plots and intentions in males who use their power to break women down. Sexual energy is a potent force for them, leading them to prioritize sex before the start of a relationship. This historical pattern is reflected in the practice of selling virgins to men.

They use their penis as a weapon of mass destruction to break women down psychologically, and this is substantiated by biology and science. Additionally, they revel in impregnating women and then abandoning them, intentionally hindering or halting their spiritual growth, fully aware that they were never going to be father or husband material. Historically, males have consistently left women to bear the burden of the relationship, while they ride off into the sunset with another woman or man. It's an uncomfortable truth that women need to confront. Becoming a real man requires significant effort from males, who often evade accountability and responsibility for their actions, even needing coercion to fulfill financial obligations like paying bills and child support. This should raise important considerations for queens, urging them to conduct thorough research and homework.

Predators are really good at manipulating important things to control and threaten you. This is very dangerous for women. It's important not to get emotionally attached to guys because it can keep women stuck and controlled by a harmful spirit, making their lives difficult for a long time. Recovering from bad relationships or marriages takes a while because the impact of predators lingers. They leave their mark everywhere they go, and eventually, you might start acting and saying things you normally wouldn't. This harmful spirit aims to take control, dominate, and harm all your desires, essentially giving it the power to break you down.

CHAPTER 5:
THE PANIC ROOM

The enemy seeks to kill, steal, and destroy. Women must be cautious of those entering their lives to take away their inner peace. Uncontrolled emotions, anxiety, over thinking, and nervousness are tools of demonic forces that manipulate fear of leaving a toxic relationship. It ensnares and pulls her back. She remains due to fear, creating a dominating spirit that drives her to the edge, draining the life out of her. Initially, it prompts her to act out of character, fostering anger and outbursts.

This situation mirrors a real-life fatal attraction, leading to a potential nervous breakdown. Involvement in violence may occur due to the soul tie and predator's DNA. Many women end up in prison or dead because of entanglement with such evil spirits, fueled by impulses and a desire for rage. Medication is not a solution to this problem. This spirit thrives on the reactions stemming from love, using torture to control the mind, body, and soul.

Experiencing pain and trauma with someone is not love. One of the biggest curses women impose on themselves is identifying as a "ride or die chick" for a male, not realizing they are literally dying in a relationship they shouldn't be in. Decision-making based on situations and circumstances can lead to misfires in spiritual discernment. Trust your God-given moral compass; it will guide you away from the path of destruction. If you find yourself in a constant panic, texting, calling, driving around searching for them, losing sleep, feeling confused, or unhappy, these are not normal behaviors.

Males often use the promise of marriage or monogamous relationships to ensnare single women. This is part of the mind games they play, aiming to entangle women emotionally. They employ gas lighting and love bombing in the initial 90 days, especially after shared intimate moments, like cooking or having sex, all while hiding their true motives. The tactic is to keep women confused, convincing them that this is the best they can achieve. Many women settle for a partner to showcase publicly when they don't love themselves enough.

The enemy repeats the cycle by sending similar demonic men season after season. When women lack self-love, they give everything to the wrong person freely. Males play mind games rooted in their insecurities, telling women they're worthless and that nobody else wants them. This is a reflection of the male's self-perception, as projection becomes their powerful weapon against women. Additionally, women should be cautious of friends offering harmful advice, especially those stuck in toxic relationships for years. These friends might know everything about their partner's wrongdoings but refuse to leave, or they might suggest praying, hoping for change.

The church often preaches and teaches women to accept struggles in love. Unfortunately, some pastors and churchgoers have given women bad advice, despite knowing they were being cheated on and abused, exposing them to potential diseases. Tragically, some women have lost their lives due to this evil spirit, leaving them trapped with no way out. It's crucial for women to prioritize their mental well-being and strive for a balanced and healthy life.

There's nothing inherently wrong with being alone or single. It's important to assertively say no at times and avoid making decisions solely based on emotions, biological clocks, or feelings of loneliness. Comparing one's life to others can be detrimental, so it's advisable to seek therapy or guidance from a spiritual advisor. The goal is to avoid a lifetime of regret stemming from poor life decisions.

WOMEN FUNDAMENTAL RIGHTS

Fundamental definition: forming a necessary base or core, of central importance.

1. you have the power and right to have a different opinion from others.
2. You have the power and right to create your own healthy and happy lifestyle.
3. you have the power and right to express your feelings, opinions, wants and needs.
4. you have the power and right to set your own priorities and standards.
5. you have the power and right to say no without feeling guilty or judged.
6. you have the power and right to be treated with respect in every relationship with family, friends, community, and partner.
7. you have the power and right to take care of and protect yourself from being threatened physically, mentally, or emotionally.
8. you have the power and right to take back everything that the enemy has stolen from you.

CHAPTER 6:
DON'T ALLOW THE DEVIL TO
THROW OFF YOUR INTUITION

A significant number, at least 70% or more, of women struggle to effectively use or operate the gift of discernment. The enemy cunningly employs spiritual gifts against intuition, particularly targeting the sharp and powerful tool that is God-given. The seven powerful gifts include having a righteous spirit, wisdom, understanding, counsel, fortitude, knowledge, piety, and fear of being in danger.

Godly intuition is a unconscious emotion originating from the body, while the brain is influenced by thoughts that might be partially right or wrong. In serious relationships, this becomes the enemy's playground, leading women through an emotional roller coaster. As a soul tie transforms, the enemy can present illusions or images to manipulate what you know and see.

To maintain control, the enemy may make you feel like abuse is a form of love. Discernment can reveal that someone is treating you poorly, yet the belief that prayer can change them may allow this evil spirit continued access to your life.

Males often exploit the open-door grace policy from women, disappearing for weeks with another woman, yet sweet-talking their way back. In the spiritual realm, he marks his territory like a dog. A toxic trait among women is the belief that she can save a man from the demons he created for himself, which is not her responsibility.

Regrettably, women might experience one good year with a man but spend 20 years attempting to recapture that one positive period, clinging to the hope that "He was not like this in the beginning." This behavior is a form of insanity, and seeking a crisis manager is crucial. Once someone reveals their true self, it's vital to believe it and swiftly leave—run as fast as you can. Some evil spirits may take longer to unveil their true nature, but narcissistic traits follow a pattern meant to deceive. The longer you stay, the more challenging it becomes to break free.

Women must establish the foundation for a healthy relationship. Discernment, an inner strength often under-estimated, holds incredible power that can shield women from unnecessary heartache and pain. Understanding this power enables women to navigate and overcome challenging thoughts effectively. In a state of bondage, a woman lacks protection, rendering her defenses weak, which is why she may permit men to take advantage of her.

In such a vulnerable state, she becomes prey for predators. The truth stands alone, while lies require many allies. Only when women comprehend the complete truth about male nature can they liberate themselves from self-imposed bondage. Merely having a piece of a man is not an accomplishment to true queens who recognize their worth and confidently walk in righteous power.

CHAPTER 7:
SERVING A LIFE SENTENCE IN A RELATIONSHIP PUTTING YOURSELF IN A SPIRITUAL PRISON

In contemporary culture, the term "life partner" is commonplace, reflecting the reality that individuals can be deeply connected to someone for a significant portion of their lives, potentially becoming entangled in a web of sin. The enemy exploits societal structures, utilizing the government to enact harmful laws that legitimize common-law marriages. (Consider, though, who you might be spiritually handcuffed to.) When individuals find comfort in chaos, they may endure years of various abuses—verbal, physical, sexual, or financial.

Entering into a covenant with a demonic soul tie is an immensely perilous game for a woman, as it results in forfeiting all rights to her soul. Some individuals have descended into the abyss of idolatry, worshiping themselves, money, or unrestrained sexual desires, rendering moral standards and values obsolete. This contagious spirit has permeated the majority of the world, where genuine love remains largely misunderstood by over 90% of the population.

Being single and embracing self-control is not the popular narrative; society often portrays a life of wildness, recklessness, and rebellion as the norm. Toxic males exhibit a sense of entitlement, evident in their rhetoric: "Let me hurt you before you hurt me," "I'll use you before you can use me," or "I'll stay as long as you accept me, playing my part because I am your weakness."

They establish a routine, acknowledging the familiarity of the cycle. When caught cheating, they downplay the severity, employing lies and manipulation to navigate through emotions. Temporary remorse may be expressed through gifts and makeup sex, creating a false sense of change. However, the repetitive cycle resumes within a few months. This trapping dynamic can include children and hinder educational pursuits, keeping individuals ensnared in a detrimental pattern.

Expressing fear that intelligence might lead to departure and admitting jealousy when a woman excels, the toxic narrative continues. The potential of losing jobs, leaving financial burdens on the partner, and secret liaisons with others underline a pattern of unfaithfulness. This toxic culture perpetuates the idea that men lack fidelity, contributing to women's entanglement in a spiritual prison.

Evil spirits, designed to consume time, energy, and peace, work to isolate and dominate, achieving control as their ultimate goal. In this scenario, the available options seem grim, with fears of leaving, handling single parenthood, or financial struggles paralyzing women into submission. This forms an unhealthy and detrimental soul tie.

Trauma bonding is a potent system designed to dismantle all of a woman's defense mechanisms. Queens, it's crucial to rid yourself of this diabolical narcissist. Understand that all he'll do is move on to a new source. Refrain from pitying a grown man; he must navigate life's challenges just like any woman.

Males with a criminal history, especially those who've been to prison, pose heightened risks. Many are on the down low, seeking vulnerable women for personal gains. Breaking free from the beast system they've created is a rarity. Let these men face their karma; believe me, the new woman is enduring their suffering. These men often search for a woman to bring them peace, but demons don't possess peace; they disrupt others' tranquility.

Without healing and wholeness, women may consistently seek love externally, and these types of men will keep returning as familiar spirits, season after season. Break free, reclaim your power; your life depends on it.

CHAPTER 8:
LOSING YOUR IDENTITY IN A TOXIC RELATIONSHIP

Jeremiah 1:5 before I formed you in the womb I knew you, before you were born I set you apart; I appointed you as a prophet to the nations.

The first thing a demonic spirit seizes is your identity, hindering independent thinking. When referencing the Bible, I utilize its scriptures from a wisdom standpoint, serving as a guide or teaching tool. The Bible, in revealing male nature, illustrates a spiritual war between males and females. Historically, women were treated as property, subjected to rape at the hands of men. However, delving deeper, many women had no choice but to comply out of fear, losing the battle from birth.

Growing up as a slave, a woman had to mature quickly, suffering an identity crisis as she relinquished her true self to shoulder adult responsibilities. When young parents neglect their duties, it places an immense burden on the woman, mentally and physically. She loses herself in her children, held back in life, while the man may move on to play house with someone else. External influences dictate her actions, words, and whereabouts.

From an early age, women become unwitting puppets for others, leading them into spiritual bondage by default. Personally raised by my grandmother, I witnessed her sacrifice her identity to care for everyone but herself. While she imparted strength, I wasn't taught how to break free from the burden of overwhelming responsibilities. Despite her selflessness, she lived a long and healthy life.

Observing such sacrifices, I've realized the toll it takes on women, contributing to family trauma and resulting in health issues like depression and high blood pressure. Many physical and spiritual diseases affecting women's bodies remain unaddressed and overlooked. There's a danger that the man a woman is involved with may contribute to her weakened and sickly state. When women meet men, the focus often revolves around the man's dreams and goals, leaving the woman waiting for promises unfulfilled and false hopes for a meaningful future.

This demonic spirit adeptly employs bread-crumbing techniques, presenting fake potential in specific areas to captivate women. Women often fall for the idealized image of who a man could become, disregarding his true character. Some men promise post-marriage improvements that never materialize, leading women to settle based on shared history. In toxic relationships, men might express dislike for a woman's friends or family, especially if they voice concerns, seeking to isolate their partner.

Toxic men aspire to keep women numb and compliant, exerting full control over their lives. These men hold archaic beliefs, confining women to traditional roles at home and as mothers. The recognition of women's freedom is crucial, as malicious men once stole their genuine rights. The resultant identity crisis represents a severe plague, threatening women's past, present, and future. Diabolical spirits have systematically robbed generations.

Women, often settling for comfort in misery, are largely unaware that their rights have been usurped by malevolent forces who have manipulated laws, government, and religion to coerce women into binding unions with demons for support and resources. A crucial step is for women to check their identity before a spirit issues a license to manipulate and control their lives.

CHAPTER 9:
RECOGNIZING YOUR STRENGTHS AND WEAKNESSES IN A RELATIONSHIP

Strength—the quality or state of being physically strong, or the capacity of an object or substance to withstand great force or pressure, power, stability resistance
Weakness—the state or condition of lacking strength or quality or feature regarded as a disadvantage or fault

It's time for women to embrace accountability in their relationships, using every experience as a valuable lesson to foster spiritual growth. Avoiding the trap of remaining stuck in a past phase requires recognizing warning signs, even if strong emotions cloud judgment. Refusing to accept, "This is just the way I am. I can't help it," is crucial, as such a mindset can lead to dangerous submission to a soul tie, particularly if influenced by misleading male perspectives.

In the realm of social media, there's a tendency to blame women for choosing poorly when hurt by men. However, it's essential to acknowledge that toxic men often employ deceit and manipulation, presenting a positive facade initially. Only when a woman lowers her guard and places trust in the relationship does the true nature of the partner become evident.

At that point, marriage, children, sexual ties, or financial entanglement may complicate matters. Unfortunately the role of religion in confusing women about male predatory nature is seldom discussed. Religious teachings often advise women to stay, not realizing that this guidance makes it harder to break away from predators with hidden agendas. These manipulative individuals adeptly shape themselves to fit your desires and ideals, becoming an integral part of your life plan.

Many women struggle to judge men's character accurately, especially when dealing with those harboring dark intentions. Some men pretend to like women while secretly harboring hatred and jealousy, seeking revenge on any woman. It's crucial to recognize the pattern and understand that even dark spirits can display sincerity, compassion, and apparent love as part of a larger plan to emotionally and spiritually ensnare you, posing a severe threat to your soul.

A lot of males are huge distractions for women in relationships. The fear of being alone makes women prey for men to destroy. It takes two dedicated partners, and that takes effort and compromise from both people, where there is no imbalance of power or respect, meaning you value who your partner is and understand each other's boundaries. What women don't know is that males operate from the waist down.

Every decision they make comes from a sexual and ego-driven purpose. That means he is going to get his needs met for free while you suffer or beg for what you want out of him in a relationship, which explains why every woman from around the world gets the same type of man, and women give men everything but, in return, the woman feels nothing but regrets on how she allowed a demon to destroy her life.

WARNING DON'T FALL FOR THE GAMES TOXIC MEN PLAY

1. Don't fall for a man who is needy or is always down on his luck, who can't keep a job, car, place or

money, or who has had multiple relationships that failed because of him.

2. Don't fall for a man who always makes excuses or believes it's never his fault.

3. Don't fall for a man who wants to control or bully and shows no respect for your morals, values, and standards, who is abusive and thinks all women are weak.

4. Don't fall for a man who is using you as a placeholder until he gets the woman he wants.

5. Don't fall for a man who has not cut off past relationships.

6. Don't fall for a man who has a lot of kids. They will be a burden on you. Pay attention to men who don't spend time or support their kids. Children need time, attention, and financial support from both parents.

7. Don't fall for a man that doesn't know his place or purpose in life. Make sure he is living the words that are coming out of his mouth.

8. Don't fall for a man who is intimidated by or jealous of your success. He will make comments or he won't show any real support or he'll distract you to keep you focused on him.

9. Don't fall for a man who doesn't spend time with you outside of sex.

10. Don't fall for a man who doesn't add value to your life. He is either an asset or a liability.

11. Don't fall in love with words or actions. Women are fooled because men lie and deceive to get their needs met for free. They will switch up and flip the script, leaving their partner confused about where she stands. (Read *The 5 Components of Love* by Princella Clark.)

12. Don't feel sorry for a man, period! He has to earn his value and success.

13. Don't fall for a man who thinks all women are the same. If he doesn't respect or like his mom, he feels the same way about you.
14. Don't fall for a womanizer who always has a new girlfriend every few months.
15. Don't fall for a man who has been in prison. He is desperate; he has nothing to lose but everything to gain. He is looking for resources from women. He needs food, shelter, sex, transportation and entertainment.
16. Don't fall for a man who pretends to like you but wants your child. Pedophiles play good stepdads in the beginning.
17. Don't fall for a man who has no self-control and who can't take constructive criticism.
18. Don't fall for a man that has a god complex.
19. Don't fall for a man who has pipe dreams to make it, flip money, or get rich quickly by selling drugs or having all kinds of crazy ideas. (Rappers and fake music careers are the worst.)
20. Don't fall for a man who downs and degrades women for social media clout to impress other men.
21. Don't fall for a man who has health issues. He will be a burden. He is looking for a caretaker. These men usually want to get married before you find out they are sick. You will be paying for everything. Studies show that men leave their wives while they are sick. 99% of them do this and they don't have health insurance. You will be in debt. Get tested for everything. Your life depends on this critical information.

CHAPTER 10:
THE SPIRIT OF STOCKHOLM SYNDROME

Sadly, all over the world, many women suffer from Stockholm syndrome without even realizing it. This phenomenon occurs when hostages or abuse victims form a bond with their captors. This demonic syndrome can take over, becoming a dominant evil spirit that perpetuates an illusion of love, which, in reality, is nothing but abuse. The enemy operates in two ways.

One manifestation involves assuming godly characteristics in a deceitful manner. As a rebellious religious cult leader, it induces a psychological breakdown, compelling victims to submit or obey. Despite sounding normal or absurd, it captivates the victim, convincing them it is harmless and drawing them in. It commands all of her attention, leading her to act out of fear. While these are subtle tactics, this is also another manifestation of a demonic narcissist with a specific assignment and agenda targeting certain types of women.

Demons seek weak women in certain areas to put them in a trance of authority and fear. You see this being displayed in a lot of religions behind closed doors. Incestuous marriage, rape, and sex trafficking are all from the mind and hands of wicked men but yet my question is why would an all knowing and powerful God put men first knowing that their true nature is evil and sinister? Men want to destroy women and bring them down to their level, so they get women to help them carry out their evil plans. How many women are stuck in relationships with men that are not going anywhere? How many married women are unhappy?

How many women find themselves with rebellious, disobedient children that they were not supposed to have, influenced by harmful forces? How many women have endured a figurative prison sentence due to their association with an evil man? These manipulative individuals often exploit women, using them to recruit others for their own purposes. A woman who doesn't recognize her worth becomes an easy target for manipulation and destruction. It's time to stop allowing good looks, charm, and deceptive personas to lead you into a living hell. That's the truth. It's time for women to awaken and acknowledge the real evil that exists in this world. To survive, it's essential to be vigilant and discerning when dealing with every man, from pastors to pimps.

CHAPTER 11:
TRAUMA UNITS

Women should take a closer look at the world and recognize that some men carry deep emotional wounds, often resembling walking, talking trauma units. A significant percentage may exhibit negative patterns in their relationships with women, stemming from a destructive criminal past. These men, influenced by the devil through generational curses and a rebellious spirit, may manipulate naive women into sympathizing with them.

This dark spirit operates with cunning deceit, presenting trauma as a twisted form of love bonding. Partners entangled with this spirit often find themselves unfairly bearing the burden of everything negative that has happened in the man's life. Whether it's the absence of parental figures, experiences of bullying, or struggles in employment, the blame is shifted onto the woman or the system. It's important for women to be aware of these dynamics and approach relationships with discernment.

This perceived demonic spirit often becomes a burden in society, lacking a clear purpose and seeking handouts without genuine contribution. These men tend to portray themselves as perpetual victims, creating their own versions of life events and twisting words to draw women into their narrative.

A man with a history of bad credit can serve as a warning sign, suggesting irresponsibility. Narcissists, skilled in manipulating women mentally, physically, and emotionally, can engage in long-term relationships due to their ability to control and break down their partners.

While it may be challenging for some men to remain faithful, it's important to recognize that not all individuals share the same behavior. Instances of cheating and dishonesty can unfortunately be common, leading women to seek companionship to avoid loneliness. Some toxic males, seeking power and importance, may manipulate women and create a destructive environment, contributing to challenges on Earth.

It's astonishing how some men blame women for broken homes, even though the man's actions often caused the breakup. Certain men display a god complex, entering relationships with a sense of entitlement and the belief that they can do no wrong, having previously mistreated people. Women frequently find themselves in challenging situations due to these individuals, resembling a spiritual hospital psych ward.

In such relationships, women often end up providing everything the man needs—shelter, money, transportation—while the man seems to consistently face challenges. Many of these men struggle with issues like substance abuse. It's essential to remember that it's not a woman's responsibility to fix, build, or compromise just to showcase having a man. Rebuilding one's life after being affected by such a spirit can take years, as the consequences of this destructive influence are enduring and challenging to overcome.

CHAPTER 12:
HAVING A SOUL TIE WITH PAIN

A woman's body often becomes a vessel for pain and trauma, providing an avenue for the enemy to exploit. This allows demonic men to attach themselves to women's lives, bringing along companions like anxiety, depression, rejection, and loneliness. The boomerang effect takes hold, drawing her back to the source for a false sense of comfort.

This is why historical and familiar spirits pose a threat to women, infiltrating through family, friends, or past lovers. Demonic predators aim to desensitize women to pain, turning them into puppets who overlook major red flags. Each time women grant demons power, they strip away joy, peace, love, self-respect, and eventually identity, leading to a spiritual coma or prison for the soul. Reclaiming everything becomes a challenging fight. When a woman's soul is locked up, it inevitably affects every aspect of her life—family, friends, career, and health.

The list of ways the enemy can use pain is extensive. It has the power to make a woman emotional or emotionally unavailable, putting demons in the driver's seat, skillfully navigating her towards a metaphorical cliff. Unfortunately, many people struggle to handle pain well, and some may end up projecting it onto others, with children often becoming unwitting victims of parental misery.

Child abuse, a common and silent killer in broken homes, is one devastating outcome of this cycle. Demons play mind tricks, causing false aches, stress, and pain, all aimed at confusing the body and making it sick. Unfortunately, many women may not recognize the spiritual source behind the pain they carry, treating it as labor and allowing it to grow into a metaphorical monster inside them over the years.

Despite these challenges, women possess the power to overcome and heal themselves. The journey begins by acknowledging self-inflicted wounds and avoiding spiritual suicide, as the first step towards personal growth and healing.

CHAPTER 13:
SELF-INFLICTED PAIN

I am not marriage material but the bigger question is are men marriage material?

This might serve as a trigger warning for some women, but let's take a moment to explore this topic. It's crucial for people to recognize that marriage isn't the ultimate goal or life dream for everyone, particularly women. Studies indicate that marriage might not provide spiritual, physical, mental, or financial benefits for women. When comparing the roles of husband and wife, it often seems that the husband has the easier end of the deal.

In today's world, being a man is not as challenging, thanks to machines and technology handling much of the heavy work. However, societal expectations often place the burden of 100% of the housework, child-rearing, and, in many cases, working outside the home squarely on women. Some women find themselves taking care of husbands who won't or can't keep a job. It's essential to acknowledge that every marriage is different, and women would be less than truthful if they claimed to have a perfect one. Examining facts and statistics can offer a more realistic perspective on the complexities of marriage.

The divorce rate is high, with the average marriage lasting only 3 to 7 years. Some women might have considered leaving years ago, but they find themselves trapped with children, bills, and dependence on their husbands for financial support, even in cases of cheating and abuse. Women often wear multiple hats in a relationship, while some men take credit as false leaders, contributing to a family dynamic that appears to be matriarchal.

In many instances, the woman becomes the cook, the mother, and even the doctor. She must maintain everyone's peace but her own, while the toxic man enjoys a more passive role. The traditional patriarchal structure, where males are prioritized, seems to contribute to women outliving men. This is attributed to men being perceived as rebellious and disobedient, which, in turn, affects mankind's overall well-being and shortens life-span. The idea that married men live longer is often linked to the assumption that having a wife helps govern and stabilize their lives.

ALL women know that men hate going to the doctor, so it's the wife behind him making any righteous decisions. Men may silently carry various health issues and even succumb to diseases without discussing them. If they show a lack of concern for their own well-being, it raises questions about their ability to care for a woman's health. Some women find themselves holding a marriage together, perhaps due to societal expectations or religious beliefs that discourage divorce. The fairytale notion of forever, especially perpetuated by religion, can be misleading.

Consider this: men often engage with church-related activities only under specific circumstances, such as being a pastor, seeking a partner, marrying in a church, experiencing a significant life event, or nearing the end of their lives. In many cases, women end up making efforts to get their husbands to attend church. While this might be true for a significant portion of males, it's essential to acknowledge that there is also a small percentage of good men.

Many males may not explicitly communicate that they are not marriage or relationship material, yet they engage with women for various needs, including sex, food, time, shelter, or energy. These transactional interactions involve being nice only to fulfill critical needs. The word "love" can be a powerful tool for men to use, masking actions that may reveal a different reality.

This isn't intended to be negative, but rather an acknowledgment that certain men have been displaying their true nature for centuries. Despite these actions, some women continue to believe in false hope. Single women may patiently wait and save themselves, only to encounter counterfeit individuals. The scarcity of genuinely good men in the world prompts questions about why an all-knowing and powerful God would send something potentially destructive. It's worth considering that women can lead peaceful lives without necessarily relying on men.

Evil men often project their fears onto women. It's these men who may find themselves alone in their final days, having damaged every relationship in their lives. When they fall ill, family or children may not come to visit. In contrast, women tend to have friends, family, and community support when facing the end of life. Interestingly, many of these reckless men don't even have life insurance policies.

At the end of the day, the choice is yours. Be cautious about the soul contracts you sign, as they have the potential to take away your peace or even your life.

CHAPTER 14:
MASTER MANIPULATION

There is a pervasive attack on women by narcissistic males who habitually blame women for everything. This dark spirit, fueled by self-hate, unloads its problems and baggage onto women, ensnaring them in relationships that lead nowhere and perpetuating years of deception that can dismantle a family. The manipulative games and mind tricks employed by these individuals gradually work in their favor.

Women often find themselves questioning their sanity, as narcissists plant seeds of doubt both within and outside the relationship, especially to those with whom they may be cheating. Master manipulators and con artists take pride in making women feel guilty for their past, present, and future mistakes. Some men, whether rich and controlling or proud and poor, wield their influence with the intention of asserting dominance, even at the expense of someone's last dollar.

For women, it can feel like a losing battle, as they may not discover the true nature of the person they are entangled with until it's too late. These men often believe they are entitled to be with multiple women and use sex as a weapon for control and destruction. Their actions are driven by a desire for self-gratification, and it's essential to be vigilant, as this dominant dark spirit has something to prove.

WOMEN'S HEALTH: IS YOUR CHECK ENGINE LIGHT ON?

There are many different types of depression:

Seasonal depression - is known clinically with a seasonal pattern in certain seasons. For some people it's during winter or a particular time or month during the year when a familiar spirit of a person, place, or thing has you bound.

Situational depression — is known as adjustment disorder with a depressed mood

Examples: the death of a loved one, a serious or life-threatening event, going through a divorce or child custody issues, being in an abusive relationship, financial difficulties

Atypical depression - known as being depressed but temporarily goes away in a positive response to positive events temporary happiness but never experiencing God's joy

Major depression - having many mental health conditions you could have everything you want and still find reasons to be unhappy. Recreational drugs and drugs prescribed by a doctor can cause depression as well because they trick your mind and body into thinking you need those things to function and be happy, a major trick of the enemy.

Persistent depression - this can last for 2 years or more and leads to chronic depression. A lot of times people don't know why they are depressed, stay confused and numb, and do not deal with life

Manic bipolar depression - hereditary can be passed down having hypomania where you may feel very happy, change, and have mood swings but will show major signs of depression

Perinatal depression - clinically known that occurs during and after pregnancy

Premenstrual dysphoric disorder (PMDD) - makes you feel emotional, anger, sadness, extreme mood swings, lack of energy

CHAPTER 15:
HAVING A SOUL TIE WITH FAMILIAR SPIRITS

Familiar spirit definition - A spirit or a demon that serves or prompts an individual

Latin familiaries meaning - a household servant because you invite this spirit in as a friend so it is harder to get it to leave

Examples of familiar spirits' characteristics

Sabotage, distraction, and finding a weakness, come to slow you down to procrastinate, reminisce about the unhealthy past, come in seasonal growth, invite itself into your life as harmless, put you in a trance or comfort zone to break you down again.

Familiar spirits are perilous, especially because they operate during critical seasons and don't hesitate to leave you in critical condition, only to return in another form claiming they've changed—often after wasting decades of your life. How many women have heard that line, either before or after 20 years have slipped away, and now he's suddenly ready for marriage? This dark spirit observes you throughout, moving in alignment with your purpose.

It takes pleasure in watching a woman's biological clock, striking at the right time to force quick decisions made on impulse. The enemy often appears before a supernatural breakthrough, seeking to kill, steal, and destroy the hard work, personal development, and healing you've undergone, pulling you back into bondage by your own choice, as you've granted demons access once again. This compromises on things you swore you'd never do again.

For many women, familiar spirits often manifest as male ex-partners who previously wronged them, wanting to reenter their lives, presenting themselves as changed individuals. They prey on women, especially those who have achieved financial stability, reappearing out of nowhere as if nothing ever happened. Reflect on how many women's lives have been impacted by one wrong decision, giving the wrong toxic man a chance, forcing them to start over repeatedly in an attempt to make up for lost time.

CHAPTER 16:
THE SPIRIT OF SABOTAGE

Self-sabotaging behavior definition - is when it creates problems in daily life and interferes with long-standing goals

Warning sabotage characteristics in males if the behavior is not broken it can be transferred to every emotional and sexual partner

Rebellion, jealousy, hypercritical, short-tempered, blaming others, depression, low self-esteem

The most common self-sabotaging behaviors include procrastination, self-medication with drugs, sex, alcohol, eating for comfort, self-injury like cutting, and having a proud spirit about hurting others and getting away with it.

It's crucial for all women to recognize the signs when a toxic man is seeking a way out of a relationship. Self-sabotaging behaviors are red flags that something is wrong with your partner. Males may cheat as a sport or hobby, gaining street credibility from other men. They might push boundaries to see how much a woman can endure before breaking down. This stress and worry can, in some cases, cause women to age prematurely.

Women may not realize that males often have a secret bro code system, discussing how to undermine women behind closed doors. The toxic behavior can manifest in lies about commitment, just to get sex for free, and later admitting they never wanted a serious relationship.

In some instances, women may find themselves pregnant or dealing with unwanted STDs due to intentional sabotage by toxic men, who see these tactics as a way to slow the woman down, not themselves. Despite the destructive behavior, some women, deeply in love, allow it to ruin their lives. Demons, who prioritize their own needs over others, manipulate and trap women by initially presenting themselves as nice.

Even if a woman has moved on, demons might return after years, claiming they have changed. It's crucial not to settle or take risks just to start over again. Consider the years a toxic man may have taken from you. Queens should never allow anyone to drain the life out of them, hinder their progress, or take credit for their destruction. Many women have lost their lives and careers waiting for a demonic man to change. The question arises: How effective were your prayers to change someone you should never have been with in the first place?

DO NOT BECOME A SINGLE MARRIED WOMAN

In the world today, statistics and data show that women initiate divorce more often than men. Seventy percent of divorces are initiated by women, but why is the question. The answer to this question is very important because the majority of women do not know that they are signing their life over to a demon in marriage. Single married women become single married mothers because the whole relationship she is contributing 100% of the work while her husband contributes the bare minimum.

She is working, taking care of the children, cooking, cleaning the home, while the man lives a soft life. He can hang with his friends, stay out late – he has no care in the world. If you look at male nature and culture, men are abusive, violent, and abandon their children all the time. They have to be forced to pay child support or even spend time with their own child.

Men hate women, especially if she tries to leave or reject him. The ID channel is dedicated to men who murder and rape. This is a huge problem. Wake up, women. Can't you see that they are the most dangerous people in the world?

The only source that claims men can be good is the Bible, but the world often reveals a stark truth. A woman can't walk down the street alone without fearing an attack, prompting the question: Was love genuinely present? How does a wife juggle so many roles? She serves as the doctor, therapist, caretaker, secretary, banker, and provider of all her husband's sexual needs, yet she still faces betrayal through infidelity.

Men cheat 99% of the time, spanning from the highest echelons to the lowest in the street. What, then, are women signing up for? It often feels like signing up to be a slave. Wives remember holidays and birthdays, handling all the planning, making the deal seem remarkably unfair.

Women frequently find themselves caught and trapped in the institution of marriage. Despite feeling exhausted and miserable, they often wear a mask to save face for the church, family, friends, and society. There's a pervasive belief that women should endure and sacrifice to maintain a marriage, regardless of the hardships.

Women worldwide have been hurt and conditioned by religious teachings, encouraging them to pray for a good husband. It's time to reevaluate: Are men truly good relationship partners, or have you been deceived by the enemy all along? Research supports the fact that women's lifespan are shorter due to the stress inflicted by marriages or relationships with toxic males. It's crucial for women to conduct thorough research on patriarchal marriage, recognizing it as a social construct crafted by wicked men to produce slaves and perpetuate generational curses. This understanding helps explain why the world faces so many challenges today.

CHAPTER 17:
THE DEMONIC SPIRIT BEHIND MASKING

MASKING

Masking definition - a process in which an individual changes or masks their natural personality to conform to social pressures, abuse, or harassment, can be strongly influenced by environmental factors such as rejection, and emotional, physical, or sexual abuse

The narcissist operates as an imposter, utilizing a significant technique known as the mirror effect in trauma bonding. This strategy aims to break a woman, compelling her to bear the majority of pressure and unnecessary weight in the relationship. This facade allows the narcissist to appear as a good person publicly, while privately, he reveals himself as a monster.

Males often feign a desire for genuine help, yet they reject therapy. Marriage, history, and long-term relationships become breeding grounds for this type of demon to thrive. The confusion it instills in women about potential solutions leaves them trapped without a clear path to leave or address the problem. The narcissist seeks justification for the toxic mess he created, which can be not only destructive but potentially deadly.

This dynamic puts women in bondage, as a man only needs to convince a woman that he has the potential to change, keeping her in the grasp of an evil spirit with two faces. People can mask various emotions while slowly deteriorating on the inside, leading to serious health issues. Staying in a dead-end situation can result in drug or alcohol abuse, fluctuations in weight, high blood pressure, and depression. The list goes on.

Consider this: How many women do you know that remained in a toxic relationship due to marriage, children, financial support, fear, or the reluctance to be alone? Many are pressured to stay, controlled, and manipulated by family, friends, church, and social media.

Public Service Announcement: Narcissistic men can successfully mask a marriage for an extended period, draining their partners of everything. They may file for divorce after the wife has contributed to their success. It's a common scenario, and many women express that the man they married was not like this in the beginning. These men often harbor a god complex, seeking importance, major titles, and high offices of respect.

Men in positions of power wield money, influence, and resources supported by governmental laws, religion, sports, or entertainment. The news has brought to light the indiscretions of men in various influential roles, spanning from the pope, president, CEO, lawyer, to the average male and the person on the streets. Their actions, whether related to embezzlement, sexual misconduct, infidelity, racism, or misogyny toward women, demonstrate a consistent lack of self-control in leadership. Centuries of history showcase this pattern.

It's worth delving into this information and doing your homework to uncover the unsettling truth about male nature. Pose this question to yourself: Who is genuinely made in God's image on this earth?

THE PLACEHOLDER WOMAN

Proverbs 14:1 - a wise woman builds her house, while a foolish woman tears hers down with her own hands.

This woman has waited patiently for years, hoping her man would change, settle down, and commit to being her husband. Unfortunately, he continually fills her head with lies and broken promises. She's his ride or die, unaware that she's more of a spare tire until he finds someone he deems better. Exploiting her willingness to prove her love, he can leave her anytime, confident in the power to return, even if he impregnated someone else or marries a side chick. This situation creates confusion and unnecessary drama, as toxic males thrive on pitting women against each other in futile competition.

He's aware that he can play both women season after season. What women must understand is that men rarely completely break off ties with other women. In many cases, it's the woman who makes the decision to sever all connections and not be in a relationship. This reality explains why men often attempt to return years later, checking if there's still a chance. Deep down, men recognize that they contribute significantly to the problem, yet they desire women to share in their suffering.

Women should understand that their husbands or boyfriends may not genuinely love them. Narcissists excel at acting, playing the role of a devoted partner for years, only to suddenly marry someone they've known for a much shorter period. Throughout history, women have often been treated as doormats, enduring draining relationships that lead nowhere. Many women sacrifice their youth, time, money, and energy, falling victim to men who use money and gifts to keep them around. It's crucial to reflect on whether you've ever been a placeholder, unknowingly giving everything to a predator until he found a supposedly better opportunity.

CHAPTER 18:
THE SPIRIT OF ENTITLEMENT

Entitlement definition: the fact of having a right to something, the belief that one is inherently deserving of privileges or special treatment

Entitlement is a toxic narcissistic trait, repeatedly exposing people to the risk of feeling frustrated, unhappy, and disappointed with life. They want to be admired and respected by everyone

Narcissistic entitlement refers to one's importance, or uniqueness. This should result in getting special treatment and receiving more resources than others.

Entitled men and women have high expectations that go unmet, and will allow people they are using to go above and beyond to please them. This can lead to disappointment and psychological distress.

Entitled individuals, both men and women, often struggle to maintain positive relationships with others. They frequently perceive treatment as unfair and may seek revenge to assert control and dominance over their partners.

Many people carry a false sense of power and entitlement, a poisonous mindset rooted in childhood experiences of never being denied, consistently acting out to achieve their desires. This behavior often instills fear in others, shaping an intimidating bully-like persona. This toxic spirit, growing up with a need to prove something, becomes particularly challenging for men who cannot handle rejection.

They believe they are entitled to a woman's service and may marry for benefits without genuine love in their hearts. This demonic culture has given rise to a nation of men who are weak, so they put others down to elevate their own status. This mindset can lead to a dangerous and potentially deadly game, especially for women perceived as beneath them. The entitled individual often blames the woman for their failures.

Entitlement, rather than being a strength, is a weakness rooted in the need to outshine others, driven by selfishness, loneliness, and jealousy. This spirit is never satisfied, controlling everything around its schedule and making everyone's life miserable. With two faces—one in the light and one in the dark—this evil spirit thrives by staying hidden, avoiding exposure.

CHAPTER 19:
THE SPIRIT OF LUST

Lust definition: having a very strong sexual desire for someone or something and intense longing craving for pleasure .

The Bible reveals male nature plainly, discussing the body as a temple and advising women to keep their virtue. Yet, one must ask: do men treat their bodies as temples? Solomon, with 700 wives and 300 side relationships, challenges the idea of wisdom, exposing a lack of control and sexual discipline.

In relationships, what might seem like love at first sight is often lust. Many mistake seasonal lust for lasting love, setting the stage for a lifetime of pain. Lust is dangerous, accompanied by a jealous and envious spirit, blurring the line between desire and animosity.

Lust, a powerful force, infiltrates the mind, body, and soul. This selfish emotion takes pride and control, wreaking havoc on relationships and communities. Unwanted pregnancies, broken homes, and disease often result from the reckless actions of individuals driven by lust, who prioritize momentary pleasure over long-term consequences.

The illusion of love accompanies these pleasurable encounters, masking the true nature of the relationships formed. Understanding male nature requires acknowledging their aversion to seeking medical attention. Many prioritize indulging in multiple relationships without considering the broader impact on themselves and others.

They will have sex with children, animals, and dolls, other men, objects and even the dead. The list goes on. Sex demons come to kill, steal, and destroy the body, mind, and soul or to put women in a lifetime of disease and depression. The allure of temptation can make lust seem enticing in the moment, but it's essential for women to recognize the trap it represents. Engaging in lust-driven experiences may lead to negative consequences, with a man using a woman for his desires and potentially harboring resentment afterward. Women must navigate these challenges and be cautious about becoming tools for someone else's satisfaction, understanding that such encounters may not lead to genuine connection or mutual respect.

Lust's cunning nature can exploit vulnerabilities, particularly when a woman lacks self-love and seeks validation through attention and kind words. The manipulative aspect of lust involves studying and understanding a woman's behavior, targeting her at vulnerable moments. The misconception that marriage cures lust is debunked by the prevalence of adultery, indicating that the underlying issues persist even within marital relationships. The dangerous consequences of lust, including violence and control, are depicted in various media, emphasizing the need for awareness and caution in relationships.

There are laws that protect men from crimes of passion because men look out for other men and they have a sick sympathy for them because they are the ones making the laws and running the government. Lust is also a spirit that will waste your time. This dark spirit has no real foundation. It's based on impulse to make a decision without real discernment or thought. Lust is a distraction to pull someone away from themselves and focus on meaningless sex and keep a woman a slave to suffer under easy access laws.

CHAPTER 20:
KNOW YOUR LIMITS

It is time for women to understand their limits and expectations in a relationship. The issue lies in women waiting a long time to see if their partner will genuinely change before they can move forward. Depending on the depth of the soul tie, women have been conditioned to remain in a serious relationship and make it work, not realizing that a demonic spirit may have established itself to wreak havoc.

Men often dangle marriage in front of women like a carrot, keeping them loyal to the idea without real intentions until they are ready. Marriage does not fundamentally alter who the man truly is. His sinister nature will inevitably surface, whether in public or behind closed doors. Women must comprehend who a man is beyond their presence. This serves as a major red flag, indicating that she is in the danger zone and at the mercy of a dominant spirit.

She has lost her true power of discernment, overlooking what's right in front of her face. Men have demonstrated that they can remain engaged for years without any genuine commitment. Males seek women they can return to after being players and running the streets. It's often a life-altering situation that prompts them to come back and prey on a woman's emotions.

They may claim to be sick or cite a family tragedy like the death of a mother for sympathy or clout, and suddenly, they're back in her life. Familiar spirits are among the most dangerous entities in the world, employing one of the oldest tricks in the book to sabotage a woman's life. Biological clocks pose a significant setback for women. Here's a news flash: this malevolent spirit already knows your worth and treats you as though you're worthless, a mere pawn to be used until something better comes along. Women possess the power to reverse the curse on them and break free from these relationship horror stories.

It's simple: stop allowing men access to you. Demons don't respect morals or high values. Sooner or later, the true mask will come off, and you must hope it's not too late, avoiding the risk of harm. As a woman, you must be highly valuable in this cruel world, never allowing a man to obtain you at a discounted price.

Life is about making difficult decisions. You cannot afford to be submissive to an artificial system designed for your failure at any cost. While no one is perfect, as a woman, you don't have the time to teach and train a grown man on respect, love, and loyalty. Healthy relationships are rare. Close all doors and chapters. Queens would never find themselves as the side chick, a slave, or stuck in a situation where they're drained emotionally and financially, just for someone else's ego boost to say, "I have a man."

CHAPTER 21:
THE SPIRITUAL BREAK UP

Predators often assume a guise that allows them to wreak havoc on women for a lifetime. When a woman reaches her breaking point, it's not just about breaking up; it's about breaking free from a vicious cycle that kept her restrained. Women should pose a critical question to themselves: Did this relationship uplift me or tear me down?

Numerous steps must be taken to ensure that evil spirits do not creep back in years later, especially if the relationship was significant—such as in marriage or with children. However, some women have so much history with a man that they can't envision a life without him. As I've mentioned before, he has marked his territory in her brain, possessing her mind, body, and soul. Even if he is no longer in a relationship with her, he still has her tethered to him through a soul contract. There are crucial steps a woman must take to break free and sever the ties of a demonic soul connection.

1. She must initiate a physical breakup with the male— no sex or contact, period. It's essential to have a strong support group or an accountability partner, maintaining a small circle free of individuals trying to share information about him. It's crucial to remember that the breakup has occurred. His whereabouts and company are no longer your concern.

2. Breaking the spiritual soul tie will require time, fasting, and prayer. Carrying someone else's demons can impact you on a deep level, and it takes time for these spirits to work on you, breaking you down chemi-

cally and trapping your natural defenses, such as discernment, making it difficult to fend them off. Evil spirits can haunt and torment you for years after that person is gone, so it's crucial to ensure complete deliverance.

3. To initiate the mental breakup, begin distancing yourself from his friends and family, as anything can trigger you right back to him. Recognize the dysfunction and embark on the healing journey from the pain of abandonment and rejection. Focus on positive aspects of life as there has been significant damage to your self-esteem. This is a process of starting over and rebuilding yourself.

4. The emotional breakup is the final spirit to release because thoughts of them persist, accompanied by flashbacks. Everything around you serves as a reminder, prompting a reflection on the good times in the beginning, yet the enemy provided a smoke screen mirror. What you thought you truly wanted and prayed for turned out to be a form of spiritual suicide. Emotions come to console your hidden trauma, and fighting this spirit becomes essential to reclaim your inner peace.

Women should pose a crucial question to themselves: Is it truly worth surrendering your life so that a demonic predator can thrive as a parasite, using you as a host to accomplish nothing but setting you back for a lifetime of regrets?

DO NOT ADOPT MALE KARMA

Women must understand the potency of negative energy and how it can transfer and permeate the mind, body, and soul. It serves as a warning sign that a woman may have unknowingly entered into a spiritual contract, destined to long-suffer with a demonic force. Toxic males embody the spirit of destruction and death, entering people's lives with the sole purpose of causing harm.

Women naturally carry pain and heartache in their wombs, so when she aligns herself with the wrong man or partner, her entire life undergoes a transformation. Her mental, physical, and emotional well-being are put at risk, and in severe cases, this could be detrimental to her health. She may observe that tasks in life, once effortless, become increasingly challenging for her to achieve.

Demonic spirits can lead to the loss of everything one has worked hard for, inducing the spirit of anxiety and depression. Some women may even experience physical manifestations, such as hair loss. In their efforts to salvage a toxic relationship or marriage, women may inadvertently subject themselves to unnecessary storms without realizing who initiated the turmoil. Women in a soul tie carry the male's DNA, absorbing their anger and frustration, ultimately lacking peace.

This message extends to the side chick: willingly involving yourself with a demonic spirit is not a display of strength. Being on the side of anything means you are no better than the demon you are associating with. When he's done draining one woman, he may come back to drain you, transferring that negative energy into your being. Women have been entangled in fights over demons with generational curses for years, resulting in broken homes and misplaced children who perpetuate the same destructive cycle. Remember, misery loves company. Do not voluntarily sign a death sentence.

PSA: The male's karma stems from living a dangerous, reckless life of destruction without purpose or desire for one. Prisons are seen as cages holding demonic spirits, released to wreak havoc on the world once set free. Trauma, disease, pain, heartache, long-suffering, and early death become the ultimate fate for such individuals. When women cosign and yoke up with this dark spirit, they inadvertently take on his karma, putting their own lives in danger.

CHAPTER 22:
THE BACKUP PLAN

Every woman must realize that she holds power in a relationship—the power to walk away without regrets. The most significant mistake a woman can make is loving the wrong man. Loyalty, faithfulness, and commitment are virtues that predators exploit, often leveraging religion to coerce a woman into cosigning her life and rights to a man solely based on his gender. It's essential to evaluate whether the partner is genuinely a good match or if the decision was made under pressure, hoping to see them as better, leading to the submission of one's life as if it were a form of servitude merely to meet societal or religious expectations. Let's delve deeper into this dynamic.

The Bible, in Ephesians 5, outlines godly characteristics for men, but the reality in the world often contradicts these ideals. Many men assert that cheating is inherent to their nature, urging women to accept it. They engage in lies and manipulation, creating a fantasy until the woman realizes she is being played. The question arises: why is it so challenging for a man to be loyal to one woman, with over 90% showing through actions that they don't want to be tied down? Continuing to put one's life on hold for nothing in return raises concerns.

If a lifestyle or marriage must be forced, it is not natural. Women seek love, while men often pursue power. The enemy has found a way to break hearts, but it's crucial to take this advice as a reality check, holding your head up, queen. Being with the wrong person may have made you a victim, but dwelling in victim mode prevents true healing, fostering bitterness and toxicity due to a lingering soul tie in your DNA. Move on and don't look back.

You bear the responsibility for your peace and healing. Carrying emotional abuse can trap you in a cycle of repetition. The Bible warns about the instability of a double-minded person, making it unpredictable when a predator might flip out or change. Some men can leave women in severe debt, causing them to lose their home, car, job, and career. They may ruin her credit, drain her of assets and resources, then move on to the next woman to repeat the same pattern.

It's disheartening how many women share similar stories, left with a load of responsibilities while the man is gone without a worry. Women should never sacrifice their dreams, education, or careers just to say they have a man. Beware of the deceptive appearance of godliness, as it can be the oldest trick to trap a woman into sacrificing herself for a relationship, while the man only seeks personal gain, clout, and fulfillment of his needs. Don't allow a predator seeking easy prey to come in, set up shop, and destroy everything you've built without him.

A BACKUP PLAN CAN SAVE YOUR LIFE.

1. A backup plan protects you.
2. A backup plan can help you reach your goals.
3. A backup plan will keep you in a position of power.
4. A backup plan keeps you ahead in life and debt-free.
5. A backup plan secures you so a predator will never have the upper hand on you.
6. A watch your debt ratio and put yourself on a budget.
7. Work on your credit; no co signing for someone else.
8. Save money in case of emergency.
9. Build wealth and income for yourself and keep it private.

CHAPTER 23:
HEALING AND FORGIVING

Healing and forgiving yourself are paramount when stepping away from a toxic, abusive relationship, whether you walk, run, or crawl. The therapeutic process of healing allows you to become whole, set free, and fulfill your true purpose in alignment with God. Spiritual healing has the potential to save your life, mending your mind, body, and soul, bringing joy and peace if you allow it into your heart.

Healing from pain and hurt is a journey of taking baby steps. Reflect on areas where you may feel weak and discover your supernatural strength. Surround yourself with wise counsel, avoiding others going through similar situations, as they might inadvertently lead you back into the trap. When the enemy observes your healing progress and well-being, it becomes the perfect opportunity to send someone in to disturb your peace, which you fought hard to regain. Remember, being in a toxic relationship can lead to various health problems, including cancers, unwanted diseases, and sometimes early death.

1. Spiritual healing gives spiritual peace to know you have made the right decision.
2. Emotional healing takes control of thoughts, emotions, and feelings.
3. Mental healing takes back the power of your mind and physical illness.
4. Physical healing taking total control over weight gain or loss, hair thinning, less sleep or more sleeping, depression, not caring about how you look, neglecting

or abusing your children & doing a sexual detox cleanse on your mind, body, and soul.

FORGIVE YOURSELF STEPS

1. Acknowledge the pain and hurt
2. Consider how the hurt and pain affected you
3. Accept that you cannot change the past and move on
4. Heal and repair the broken pieces; take as much time as you need
5. Learn from your mistakes and patterns that you need to change and grow from

REFERENCES

Biblical Encyclopedia

The Holy Bible NIV (New International Version)

Psychology Of Humans And Animals YouTube: The High Powered Podcast

WomensHealth.Org

Web Md Male Biology Wikipedia, Britannica

NOTES